Sports and Activities

Let's Play Soccer!

by Heather Adamson

Consulting Editor: Gail Saunders-Smith, PhD

Consultant: Kymm Ballard, MA
Physical Education, Athletics, and Sports Medicine Consultant
North Carolina Department of Public Instruction

Capstone
press

Mankato, Minnesota

Pebble Plus is published by Capstone Press,
151 Good Counsel Drive, P.O. Box 669, Mankato, Minnesota 56002.
www.capstonepress.com

1 2 3 4 5 6 11 10 09 08 07 06

Library of Congress Cataloging-in-Publication Data
Adamson, Heather, 1974—
    Let's Play Soccer! / by Heather Adamson
       p. cm —(Pebble Plus. Sports and Activities)
    Includes bibliographical references and index.
    ISBN-13: 978-0-7368-5363-7 (hardcover)
    ISBN-10: 0-7368-5363-4 (hardcover)
    1. Soccer—Juvenile literature. I. Title. II. Series.
GV943.25.A33 2006
796.334—dc22   2005017464

Summary: Simple text and photographs present the skills, equipment, and safety concerns of playing soccer.

Credits
Kia Adams, designer; Kelly Garvin, photo researcher

Photo Credits
Capstone Press/Karon Dubke, 1, 5, 6–7, 9, 11, 13, 14–15, 16–17; TJ Thoraldson Digital Photography, cover
Corbis/Jim Cummins, 18–19
Getty Images Inc./Ty Allison, 21

Note to Parents and Teachers

The Sports and Activites set supports national physical education standards related
to recognizing movement forms and exhibiting a physically active lifestyle. This book
describes and illustrates soccer. The images support early readers in understanding the
text. The repetition of words and phrases helps early readers learn new words. This book
also introduces early readers to subject-specific vocabulary words, which are defined in
the Glossary section. Early readers may need assistance to read some words and to use
the Table of Contents, Glossary, Read More, Internet Sites, and Index sections of the book.

Table of Contents

Playing Soccer

Kick, pass, score, cheer!
Friends play soccer
as a team.

Soccer players kick the ball.
They bump it
with their heads.
They do not use their hands.

Soccer players work together

to score goals.

They dribble the ball.

They pass. They shoot.

Goalies guard the goal.

They stop the ball

any way they can.

They can even

use their hands.

Equipment

Soccer balls are made
tough for kicking.
Strong patches stitched tightly
keep soccer balls round.

Soccer fields are flat
with a goal on each end.
Players have lots of room
to run.

Soccer Safety

Soccer players protect
their legs.
They wear shin pads
under their long socks.

Following the rules keeps

everyone safe.

Soccer players are careful

not to hit or trip.

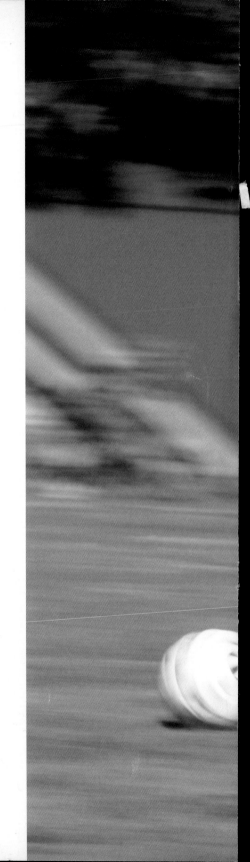

Having Fun

Come kick, bump, pass,

and score.

Let's play soccer!

Glossary

dribble—to move the ball down the field using small, short kicks

goal—a frame with a net into which teams try to kick the ball; teams score a "goal" or point when the ball enters the goal.

goalie—a player who guards the goal and tries to keep the other team from scoring

pass—to kick, throw, or hit a ball to someone on your team

patch—a small piece; traditional soccer balls are made with 32 black and white leather patches.

rule—an instruction telling people what to do

shin—area of the leg between the ankle and knee

shoot—to try to score by aiming and kicking the ball

trip—to make someone stumble or fall down

Read More

Eckart, Edana. *I Can Play Soccer.* Sports. New York: Children's Press, 2002.

Fauchald, Nick. *Score! You Can Play Soccer.* Game Day. Minneapolis: Picture Window Books, 2004.

Klingel, Cynthia Fitterer, and Robert B. Noyed. *Soccer.* Wonder Books. Chanhassen, Minn.: Child's World, 2001.

Internet Sites

FactHound offers a safe, fun way to find Internet sites related to this book. All of the sites on FactHound have been researched by our staff.

Here's how:

1. Visit *www.facthound.com*

2. Type in this special code **0736853634** for age-appropriate sites. Or enter a search word related to this book for a more general search.

3. Click on the **Fetch It** button.

FactHound will fetch the best sites for you!

Index

Word Count: 129
Grade: 1
Early-Intervention Level: 14